Major US Historical Wars

The Korean War

John Ziff

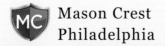

Mason Crest
Philadelphia

Mason Crest
450 Parkway Drive, Suite D
Broomall, PA 19008
www.masoncrest.com

© 2016 by Mason Crest, an imprint of National Highlights, Inc.

Printed and bound in the United States of America.

CPSIA Compliance Information: Batch #MUW2015. For further information, contact Mason Crest at 1-866-MCP-Book.

3 5 7 9 8 6 4 2

Library of Congress Cataloging-in-Publication Data

ISBN: 978-1-4222-3356-6 (hc)
ISBN: 978-1-4222-8596-1 (ebook)

Major US Historical Wars series ISBN: 978-1-4222-3352-8

About the Author: Writer and editor John Ziff lives near Philadelphia.

Picture Credits: courtesy Dwight D. Eisenhower Library: 53; Everett Collection: 19, 31; Library of Congress: 10, 17, 21 (left, center); National Archives: 22, 25, 26, 27, 28, 33, 34, 35, 37, 39, 43, 45, 48, 50, 51; © OTTN Publishing: 9; used under license from Shutterstock, Inc.: 21 (right); Traci Law / Shutterstock.com: 7; courtesy of Harry S. Truman Library: 24, 36; United Nations photo: 14, 16, 23, 38; U.S. Air Force photo: 11, 40, 46, 54, 55, 56; U.S. Military Academy at West Point: 49; U.S. Naval History and Heritage Command: 12.

Table of Contents

KEY ICONS TO LOOK FOR:

Words to Understand: These words with their easy-to-understand definitions will increase the reader's understanding of the text, while building vocabulary skills.

Sidebars: This boxed material within the main text allows readers to build knowledge, gain insights, explore possibilities, and broaden their perspectives by weaving together additional information to provide realistic and holistic perspectives.

Research Projects: Readers are pointed toward areas of further inquiry connected to each chapter. Suggestions are provided for projects that encourage deeper research and analysis.

Text-Dependent Questions: These questions send the reader back to the text for more careful attention to the evidence presented there.

Series Glossary of Key Terms: This back-of-the book glossary contains terminology used throughout this series. Words found here increase the reader's ability to read and comprehend higher-level books and articles in this field.

Other Titles in This Series

Introduction

By Series Consultant
Lt. Col. Jason R. Musteen

Lt. Col. Jason R. Musteen is a U.S. Army Cavalry officer and combat veteran who has held various command and staff jobs in Infantry and Cavalry units. He holds a PhD in Napoleonic History from Florida State University and currently serves as Chief of the Division of Military History at the U.S. Military Academy at West Point. He has appeared frequently on the History Channel.

Why should middle and high school students read about and study America wars? Does doing so promote militarism or instill misguided patriotism? The United States of America was born at war, and the nation has spent the majority of its existence at war. Our wars have demonstrated both the best and worst of who we are. They have freed millions from oppression and slavery, but they have also been a vehicle for fear, racism, and imperialism. Warfare has shaped the geography of our nation, informed our laws, and it even inspired our national anthem. It has united us and it has divided us.

Valley Forge, the USS *Constitution*, Gettysburg, Wounded Knee, Belleau Wood, Normandy, Midway, Inchon, the A Shau Valley, and Fallujah are all a part of who we are as a nation. Therefore, the study of America at war does not necessarily make students or educators militaristic; rather, it makes them thorough and responsible. To ignore warfare, which has been such a significant part of our history, would not only leave our education incomplete, it would also be negligent.

For those who wish to avoid warfare, or to at least limit its horrors, understanding conflict is a worthwhile, and even necessary, pursuit. The American author John Steinbeck once said, "all war is a symptom of man's failure as a thinking animal." If Steinbeck is right, then we must think. And we must think about war. We must study war with all its attendant horrors and miseries. We must study the heroes and the villains. We must study the root causes of our wars, how we chose to fight them, and what has been achieved or lost through them. The study of America at war is an essential component of being an educated American.

Still, there is something compelling in our military history that makes the study not only necessary, but enjoyable, as well. The desperation that drove Washington's soldiers across the Delaware River at the end of 1776 intensifies an exciting story of American success against all odds. The sailors and Marines who planted the American flag on the rocky peak of Mount Suribachi on Iwo Jima still speak to us of courage and sacrifice. The commitment that led American airmen to the relief of West Berlin in the Cold War inspires us to the service of others. The stories of these men and women are exciting, and they matter. We should study them. Moreover, for all the suffering it brings, war has at times served noble purposes for the United States. Americans can find common pride in the chronicle of the Continental Army's few victories and many defeats in the struggle for independence. We can accept that despite inflicting deep national wounds and lingering division, our Civil War yielded admirable results in the abolition of slavery and eventual national unity. We can celebrate American resolve and character as the nation rallied behind a common cause to free the world from tyranny in World War II. We can do all that without necessarily promoting war.

In this series of books, Mason Crest Publishers offers students a foundation for the study of American wars. Building on the expertise of a team of accomplished authors, the series explores the causes, conduct, and consequences of America's wars. It also presents educators with the means to take their students to a deeper understanding of the material through additional research and project ideas. I commend it to all students and to those who educate them to become responsible, informed Americans.

Chapter 1

Roots of a Forgotten War

I t raged for three years and claimed more than 35,000 American lives. Yet the Korean War occupies a dim place in the nation's collective memory. It has often been called "the Forgotten War."

Overshadowed

In part, Korea has simply been overshadowed by the wars the United States fought immediately before and after—World War II and the Vietnam War, respectively. World War II was the largest conflict in human history. Vietnam bitterly divided the American public and led to an erosion of trust in the government. Both wars continue to provide fertile grounds for inquiry by historians. Both are subjects of continuing fascination for the general public.

Even while it was going on, the Korean War failed to galvanize the country in the way World War II had, or the way Vietnam later would. In fact, a popular newsmagazine first described Korea as a "forgotten war" in the fall of 1951—nearly two years before the fighting actually ended.

Various factors explain why Americans paid scant attention to the Korean War. Unlike World War II, a "total war" that affected almost everyone in the country, Korea was a limited war. It didn't require full mobilization of the nation's young men. It didn't require a massive infusion of women into the civilian workforce. There was no rationing on the home front. The war was fought in a distant land that few Americans knew much, if anything, about. And at the time, broadcast television was still in its infancy, so people didn't see the kinds of shocking images that the nightly news would bring into American living rooms during the Vietnam War.

For its part, the U.S. government sent mixed signals about the significance of the Korean War. Breaking with longstanding practice, President

 WORDS TO UNDERSTAND IN THIS CHAPTER

annex—to incorporate a country or territory within a larger state.

capitalism—an economic system that permits the ownership of private property and allows individuals and companies to compete for their own economic gain.

communism—a political and economic system that champions the elimination of private property, promotes the common ownership of goods, and typically insists that the Communist Party has sole authority to govern.

superpower—an extremely powerful state; one of the few states that dominate an era.

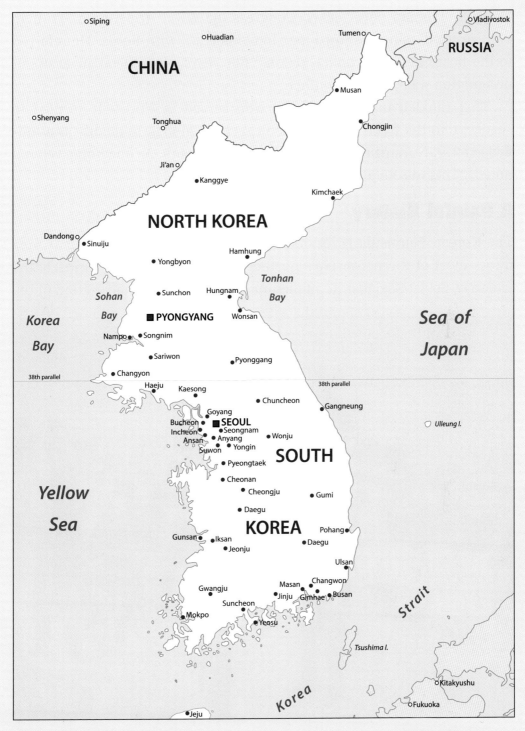

This map shows the Korean Peninsula, which was divided at the 38th parallel into northern and southern zones at the end of World War II. Place-names on this map reflect contemporary transliteration of Korean. Busan, for example, was rendered as Pusan during the Korean War; Incheon was formerly spelled Inchon.

Harry S. Truman never asked Congress for a war declaration. Truman even resisted using the word *war* in connection with Korea. He referred to the hostilities as a "police action." For years, the official government designation was "Korean conflict."

That rankled many Americans who served in Korea. It seemed to suggest that the fighting there wasn't serious enough to qualify as a full-fledged war. Nothing could be further from the truth. As one Korea veteran noted, "This was an all-out war."

A Painful History

The Korean Peninsula is located along the eastern coast of Asia. China forms most of the peninsula's northern boundary. Russia (formerly the Union of Soviet Socialist Republics, or USSR) abuts a small section of the

This Japanese print shows the Russians surrendering Chemulpo (later called Inchon) to Japanese forces in 1904. In the background on the right is the city's 40-foot-high seawall, a formidable obstacle for attacking armies.

peninsula in the far northeast. Japan lies to the east, across the Sea of Japan.

Throughout history, Korea has often been dominated by powerful neighbors. Competition for influence on the Korean Peninsula helped spark a war between Japan and Russia in 1904. Japan triumphed. In 1905, it made Korea a Japanese protectorate (a weak state that is protected and partly controlled by a stronger state). Koreans didn't particularly want that status. Many took up arms against the Japanese. Within five years, more than 17,000 had been killed.

In 1910, Japan *annexed* Korea under a treaty it forced the Korean emperor to sign. Japan's emperor, the treaty said, would reign over Korea "completely and forever."

The Japanese ruled the Korean colony harshly. They took a great deal of land from Koreans and transferred it to Japanese immigrant farmers or Japanese landlords. Many Korean families were plunged into poverty as a result. But it was Japan's efforts to expand its overseas empire that would have the most wrenching consequences for Koreans.

In July 1937, Japan invaded China. Shortly afterward, the Japanese began taking steps to suppress Korean culture and instill loyalty to Imperial Japan. These steps included compelling Koreans to adopt Japanese names, introducing Japanese textbooks into schools, and making students pledge allegiance to Japan's emperor.

In December 1941, Japanese forces attacked the U.S. naval base in Pearl Harbor, Hawaii. This pulled the United States into World War II. During the war, Japan's treatment of Koreans became more brutal. Tens of thousands of young women were abducted and made to serve as sex slaves for Japanese soldiers. Korean men were forced to provide labor, often under appalling conditions, to support the

A Honolulu, Hawaii, newspaper reports the Japanese attack on Pearl Harbor. By crippling the U.S. Pacific Fleet, Japan was able to quickly conquer a large part of the Pacific and Asia.

Japanese war effort. Japan eventually began conscripting Koreans into its army.

Japan Defeated, Korea Divided

By the summer of 1945, World War II was nearing an end. Nazi Germany had surrendered in May, bringing the war in Europe to a close. Japan continued to fight on, but its strategic situation was hopeless.

In July, the United States successfully tested a terrible new weapon: the atomic bomb. On August 6, a single atomic bomb dropped from an American warplane destroyed the Japanese city of Hiroshima.

Two days later, the USSR (which was also called the Soviet Union) declared war on Japan. Soviet troops poured into Manchuria, a Japanese-occupied region in northeastern China. While it had fought against Nazi Germany, the Soviet Union had previously honored a neutrality pact with Japan.

On August 9, the United States dropped another atomic bomb. This one obliterated the city of Nagasaki. Hirohito, Japan's emperor, announced his nation's surrender on August 15.

American officials were concerned that Soviet forces would move south from Manchuria and occupy the entire Korean Peninsula. The United States proposed that Korea temporarily be divided into Soviet and

Japanese officials arrive on the battleship USS Missouri to sign the official surrender documents ending the Second World War, September 15, 1945. The United States and its allies arranged for Japanese soldiers in Asian territories that they had captured to surrender to the nearest Allied forces. In the northern zone of Korea, the Soviets accepted the surrender, while U.S. troops controlled the southern zone.

American sectors of occupation, with the dividing line at a latitude of 38°N. Japanese troops north of the 38th parallel would surrender to the Soviets. Japanese troops south of the 38th parallel would surrender to the Americans. The Soviet Union agreed to the arrangement.

Fear of Spreading Communism

Although the United States and the Soviet Union had been allies in the fight against Nazi Germany, cracks had already begun to emerge in their relationship. Perhaps that shouldn't have been too surprising. The two countries' political and economic systems were at odds with each other.

The United States had a democratic form of government and an economy based on *capitalism*. Capitalism emphasizes private ownership of businesses, and it allows individuals to accumulate as much wealth and property as they are able. The Soviet Union, by contrast, was founded on a theory called *communism*. It says that capitalism inevitably leads to the exploitation of workers. Communism predicts that workers will revolt and overthrow the capitalist system, with the eventual result being a society in which there is no private property and in which economic goods are shared fairly. In the political sphere, communism holds that democracy is merely a tool of capitalists. Soviet leaders insisted that only the Communist Party had a right to govern.

In the immediate aftermath of World War II, U.S. policy makers worried that the Soviet Union was seeking to impose communism on other countries. The Soviets already appeared to be laying the groundwork for that in Eastern Europe. U.S. officials were determined not to allow the Soviets a free hand in Korea. Partition of the peninsula, and the arrival of American troops, would prevent the Soviets from installing a puppet regime there.

Signs of Trouble

The partition of Korea was viewed as a temporary measure, however. Soviet and American leaders alike anticipated that Korea would eventually be united under a single independent government.

Korea's future was on the agenda when the foreign ministers of the Soviet Union, the United States, and the United Kingdom met at the

Moscow Conference in December 1945. The ministers approved the creation of the U.S.-U.S.S.R. Joint Commission on Korea. It was charged with developing recommendations for the formation of a provisional (temporary) Korean government. In preparation for its full independence, Korea would be administered as a "trusteeship." Four foreign powers—the USSR, the United States, the United Kingdom, and China—would share supervisory control of Korea for a period of up to five years.

Many Koreans bitterly opposed the idea of trusteeship. They believed they were ready for self-government immediately. In fact, in early September—before the arrival of the first American troops—a prominent Korean leader named Yo Un-hyung had organized a 1,000-delegate national assembly. The assembly set up a government, the "Korean People's Republic." Its officials represented a diversity of political views. But while the Soviets quickly accepted the government as legitimate, the United States did not. General John R. Hodge, commander of American occupation forces in Korea, ordered the Korean People's Republic disbanded.

Members of the United Nations Temporary Commission on Korea discuss the future of Korea in 1948. Pictured are (left to right) S. H. Jackson of Australia, Rufino Luna of the Philippines; George S. Patterson of Canada, the chairman of UNTCOK; Coert Binnerts, principal secretary; Hung Ti Chu, secretary; Bahadur Singh of India; J. Paul-Bouncour of France; Miguel Angel Pena Valle of El Salvador, and W. Liu of China.

In the U.S. occupation zone, a host of competing political parties sprang up. North of the 38th parallel, the Soviets squeezed out all rivals to the Korean Communist Party.

A Matter for the UN?

Meanwhile, the U.S.-U.S.S.R. Joint Commission on Korea failed to agree on steps for the establishment of a provisional Korean government. The Soviets insisted that only Koreans who accepted trusteeship should be eligible to participate in the creation of a provisional government. American negotiators balked. The Communists were virtually the only Korean political party that didn't object to trusteeship.

In late 1947, with the Joint Commission at loggerheads, the United States brought the Korea issue to the United Nations. The international organization established its own commission. The United Nations Temporary Commission on Korea (UNTCOK) was charged with overseeing elections to create a free, independent, and unified Korea.

However, the Soviet Union denied that the UN had any authority to intervene in the Korea issue. The Soviets refused to permit UNTCOK officials north of the 38th parallel. UNTCOK's nine members recommended that elections proceed anyway in the American-occupied south. The winner, the commission said, should be considered the legitimate government of all Korea.

Even in the south, many Koreans vehemently opposed elections under those conditions. Labor groups, Communists, and left-leaning political parties organized protests. In April 1948, an armed uprising broke out on Jeju Island. A year would pass, and thousands of people would be killed, before that rebellion had finally been put down.

Rivals

Despite the unrest, the UN-sponsored elections went forward. In May 1948, voters in the South elected representatives to a legislature, the National Assembly. One-third of its seats were left unfilled, to allow for representation from the North if elections were held there.

The National Assembly wrote a constitution for a democratic republic and picked Dr. Syngman Rhee to serve as its president. Rhee had, for sev-

Koreans cast votes in the first free election in the history of Korea. UNTCOK supervised the election in the southern zone, which was held in May of 1948.

eral years during the Japanese occupation, headed a government-in-exile based in China. He was well known to American officials. He'd received a PhD from Princeton University and had spent many years in the United States advocating for Korean independence. He was also rabidly anticommunist.

From the American perspective, that last fact was key. In the years since the end of World War II, the mutual suspicion between the United States and the USSR had devolved into open antagonism. The two ***superpowers*** were now locked in a bitter political struggle known as the Cold War. It would last for more than four decades. During that time, the United States and the Soviet Union avoided fighting each other directly. Other than that, however, there were few limits on what the superpowers would do to increase their own influence around the world, or to undermine their adversary.

American policy makers were willing to overlook many faults in a foreign leader who took a hard line against communism. Syngman Rhee would eventually test the wisdom of that approach.

On August 15, 1948, Rhee was formally inaugurated president of the newly established Republic of Korea (ROK). The ROK claimed to be the legitimate government of all Korea.

That claim was met with derision north of the 38th parallel. Within a month, a separate state, the Democratic People's Republic of Korea (DPRK), had been proclaimed there. The DPRK's Communist government was supported by the Soviet Union and headed by a onetime guerrilla leader named Kim Il Sung.

The United States supported the government of Syngman Rhee (1875–1965) because he was strongly opposed to communism.

Festering Problems

In late 1948, the United States began withdrawing its troops from South Korea. By June 1949, the American presence had been reduced from about 50,000 to a few hundred. The remaining Americans were military advisers. Their mission was to help train the ROK's defense forces.

The Soviet Union also withdrew its occupation troops from North Korea after the founding of the DPRK. At the time, the U.S.-USSR Cold War rivalry was focused squarely on Europe. Soviet leader Joseph Stalin showed little inclination to risk a confrontation with the United States over the Korean Peninsula. Stalin seemed ready to accept a U.S. ally in South Korea as long as the Soviet Union had an ally in North Korea. American officials, too, were amenable to keeping the peninsula partitioned.

The same could not be said of Kim Il Sung or Syngman Rhee. Both men vowed to unify the entire peninsula under their leadership. The two hurled threats and accusations at each other. Rhee blamed North Korea for sponsoring a pair of violent rebellions against his government (in fact, the rebellions were nurtured by anger at Rhee's increasingly repressive regime). Kim accused South Korea of sending small military units and saboteurs across the 38th parallel. Nasty firefights erupted frequently along the border.

If not for the United States and the USSR, these provocations might easily have ignited a full-scale war. Rhee had no hope of defeating North Korea, as the United States refused to supply his government with offensive weaponry like tanks, aircraft, and heavy artillery. The Soviet Union did outfit North Korea's armed forces with such weapons. However, Stalin repeatedly denied Kim permission to invade South Korea. That would change in 1950.

 TEXT-DEPENDENT QUESTIONS

1. Which country occupied Korea from 1910 until 1945?
2. What is the 38th parallel? What significance does it have for Korea?
3. What was the Cold War?

 RESEARCH PROJECT

Choose either Kim Il Sung or Syngman Rhee. Read about his life and write a one-page profile.

Chapter 2

North Korean Onslaught

On January 12, 1950, Secretary of State Dean Acheson delivered a speech before the National Press Club in Washington, D.C. The speech dealt with U.S. policy in Asia.

Recent events lent that subject special importance. The previous October, after his forces prevailed in a civil war, Chinese Communist leader Mao Zedong had proclaimed the People's Republic of China. Communism had spread to the world's most populous country.

Soldiers of the Republic of Korea (South Korea) stand at attention during an inspection, 1950. The South Korean army was taken by surprise when North Korean forces crossed the 38th parallel on June 25, 1950.

In his speech, Acheson said the United States would maintain a "defensive perimeter" against Communist aggression in the Asia-Pacific region. That perimeter, he said, extended southwest from Alaska's Aleutian Island chain, through Japan and the Ryukyu Islands, and to the Philippines. The United States guaranteed the security of the areas on the defensive line. Any attack there would trigger an American military response.

"So far as the military security of other areas in the Pacific is concerned," Acheson noted, "it must be clear that no person can guarantee these areas against military attack." In the event of aggression outside the U.S. security perimeter, the secretary of state said, "the initial reliance must be on the people attacked to resist it and then upon the commitments of the entire civilized world under the Charter of the United Nations."

At the time he delivered it, nothing about Acheson's speech seemed especially controversial. Later, though, critics would point to one fact: Korea was outside the defensive perimeter Acheson had delineated. This, the critics said, created the impression that the United States wouldn't come to the aid of South Korea if the latter were attacked.

A Green Light from Moscow

In April 1950, Kim Il Sung traveled to Moscow to meet with Joseph Stalin. Kim pressed the Soviet leader to approve an invasion of South Korea.

 WORDS TO UNDERSTAND IN THIS CHAPTER

atrocity—a monstrous or extremely cruel act.

casualties—in war, the tally of combatants who are killed, wounded, captured, or missing in action.

GI—an enlisted person in the armed forces of the United States, especially the army.

United Nations Command (UNC)—the UN forces in the Korean War.

veto—to refuse to approve; prohibit.

North Korea's communist leader Kim Il Sung (left) sought assistance from Korea's Communist neighbors, the Soviet Union and China. Soviet leader Joseph Stalin (center) did not want his country drawn into a war with the United States, and he promised only covert assistance. Mao Zedong (right), the leader of Communist China, was willing to commit troops from his country, but Kim initially declined the offer.

Stalin had rejected the idea several times before. Now, however, he gave his assent.

Like Kim, Stalin had come to believe the United States wouldn't intervene in a war between North and South Korea. Still, he remained wary of provoking the Americans. Although he directed Soviet generals to plan North Korea's invasion, and although Soviet military personnel would train the North Korean troops, Stalin was determined to keep his country's role in the operation from coming to light. Committing Soviet combat troops was out of the question. "If you should get kicked in the teeth I shall not lift a finger," Stalin warned Kim Il Sung. "You have to ask Mao for all the help."

Kim did meet with Mao Zedong, but he declined Mao's offer to provide troops from the People's Republic of China. Kim didn't think his invasion would need any outside help to succeed. At most, he believed, it would take a few weeks for his forces to overcome South Korean resistance. In part, this optimism was based on Kim's belief that the majority of South Koreans would actually welcome the invasion. Many, he thought, would rise up to take part in overthrowing Syngman Rhee's unpopular regime.

Invasion

At dawn on June 25, 1950, North Korean troops poured across the 38th parallel. Caught by surprise, outnumbered, and outgunned, South Korean forces defending the border were quickly overrun.

North Korean units pierced the border in many places. But the bulk of the 135,000-man invasion force was concentrated in the western part of the peninsula. That's where Seoul, South Korea's capital city, was situated. It lay just 35 miles south of the 38th parallel.

News of the North Korean invasion came as a shock to American officials. The United States requested an emergency meeting of the United Nations Security Council, which quickly adopted Resolution 82. It called for an immediate cessation of hostilities in Korea and demanded that North Korean forces withdraw to the 38th parallel.

As a permanent member of the Security Council, the USSR could have **vetoed** the resolution. Since the beginning of the year, however, the Soviet Union had been boycotting the Security Council. The Soviets were protesting the UN's recognition of the Nationalist regime in Taiwan—rather than the Communist People's Republic—as the legitimate government of China.

In any event, North Korea didn't heed the Security Council resolution. It continued to press the attack.

The ROK's forces were in complete disarray. They were being shredded by North Korean artillery. They had no way to stop the enemy's

Soviet diplomat Jacob Malik casts a dissenting vote in January 1950 as the UN Security Council votes 8-2 to recognize the Nationalist government on Taiwan as the legitimate representative of the Chinese people. Angry at this decision, the USSR refused to participate in subsequent Security Council votes, which in June 1950 allowed that body to pass resolutions authorizing the use of military force in Korea.

Korean refugees flee toward the southern corner of the peninsula, away from attacking North Korean forces, 1950.

Soviet-made tanks. And their top commanders weren't exercising any tactical coordination.

Syngman Rhee blustered that the ROK army must defend Seoul to the last man. But on June 27, the president himself—along with members of his cabinet—fled the capital aboard a special train.

Tens of thousands of frightened civilians also fled southward ahead of the advancing North Koreans. Unlike their leaders, though, almost all of them had to walk or, if they were lucky, ride on an ox-pulled cart.

North Korean troops captured Seoul on June 28. **Atrocities** began almost immediately. North Korean soldiers rampaged through the National University Hospital, killing doctors, nurses, and patients alike. That slaughter, which claimed some 900 lives, hinted at the pitiless manner in which civilians would be treated throughout the war.

By no means did the Communists have a monopoly on war crimes. In fact, around the time North Korean soldiers were murdering everyone they found in the National University Hospital, South Korean forces

In a June 27, 1950, statement announcing that U.S. troops would defend South Korea, President Harry S. Truman said, "The attack upon Korea makes it plain beyond all doubt that Communism has passed beyond the use of subversion to conquer independent nations and will now use armed invasion and war."

began implementing an order President Rhee had issued the previous day. It called for the execution of South Korean civilians suspected of harboring Communist sympathies or opposing Rhee's regime. Eventually, at least 100,000 people would be killed in what came to be called the Bodo League massacre.

The UN Decides to Intervene

On June 27, the UN Security Council approved a measure to check North Korea's ongoing invasion. Resolution 83 recommended that UN member states "furnish such assistance to the Republic of Korea as may be necessary to repel the armed attack and to restore international peace and security in the area."

The United States, which had spearheaded the passage of Resolution 83, was one of 16 nations that agreed to supply combat forces to aid South Korea. Thus, for the first time in the Cold War, Americans would be fighting directly to contain communism.

 FAST FACT

In all, 20 countries answered the UN's call to come to the aid of South Korea. The United States contributed about 90 percent of the UN combat forces, but Great Britain, Canada, France, Belgium, South Africa, New Zealand, the Netherlands, Turkey, Greece, Colombia, Ethiopia, Thailand, the Philippines, and Luxembourg also sent fighting units. Denmark, Norway, Sweden, Italy, and India chipped in with medical personnel and hospital facilities.

Conditions could hardly have been less favorable for the United States and its UN allies. "If the best minds in the world had set out to find us the worst possible location to fight this damnable war politically and militarily," Dean Acheson noted ruefully, "the unanimous choice would have been Korea." Politically, Syngman Rhee was a troublesome ally, and Korea itself had little strategic importance. Militarily, Korea's geography negated many American technological advantages. The narrowness of the peninsula, a paucity of roads, and mountainous terrain hindered effective movement by a modern mechanized army like that of the United States. As a result, the numerical superiority of Communist forces would often prove decisive.

A Commander

Although the United States started providing air support for the South Koreans on June 27, it wasn't until the beginning of July that the first American ground forces arrived. By that time, after just a week of fighting, ROK troop strength had been reduced from about 95,000 men to slightly more than 20,000.

Soldiers of the Republic of Korea haul an antitank gun as they retreat from Suwon in the face of the North Korean onslaught, June 1950.

The top American military leaders in Korea included General Douglas MacArthur, who is seated in the front of the jeep, and Lieutenant General Matthew B. Ridgway, who is seated behind MacArthur. Major General Doyle Hickey, seated next to Ridgway, played an important role in planning UN operations during the Korean War.

Another Security Council resolution, passed on July 7, put all UN forces in Korea—called the **United Nations Command**, or UNC—under the unified command of the United States (Rhee would soon place ROK troops under U.S. command as well). The resolution also called on the United States to designate a commander-in-chief for the UNC. President Truman quickly announced his choice for that position: General Douglas MacArthur.

MacArthur was one of only a handful of U.S. Army officers ever to attain the rank of five-star general. To say he was a popular figure would be an understatement. Many Americans regarded him as a living legend. During World War II, MacArthur had led the victorious U.S. campaign against the Japanese in the western Pacific. It was MacArthur who accepted Japan's formal surrender in September 1945. Later, in his role as supreme Allied commander in occupied Japan, he deftly oversaw the rebuilding of the devastated Japanese economy and paved the way for a democratic system of government.

Although possessed of a first-rate military mind and an undeniable gift for leadership, MacArthur had significant flaws. He was extremely conceited. His huge ego often prevented him from considering perspectives different from his own. He was dismissive of people who questioned his assumptions or his plans. Those faults would produce tragic consequences in Korea.

American Troops Enter the Fight

If the North Koreans managed to drive all the way to the southern tip of the peninsula, the war would effectively be over. So the first task facing MacArthur and his staff was to slow the Communist onslaught long enough to permit the establishment of defensible positions.

The nearest American troops—four divisions from the U.S. Eighth Army—were in Japan. Most of these troops were rushed to Korea during the first three weeks of July 1950. They were ill prepared for what awaited.

In nearly five years as a peacetime occupation force in Japan, the Eighth Army's combat readiness had deteriorated severely. All of its divisions were undermanned. None had a full complement of armor or artillery. Weapons and equipment were in disrepair. Worst of all, training had been grossly neglected.

U.S. troops first engaged the North Koreans on July 5. Near the village of Osan, about 30 miles south of Seoul, a 540-man advance force from the 24th Infantry Division fought a delaying action against an enemy column

These African-American soldiers of the 24th Infantry Regiment were among the first U.S. troops in Korea.

U.S. Marines fire rockets at advancing North Korean forces.

consisting of three dozen tanks and approximately 5,000 soldiers. The **GI**s suffered heavy **casualties** before pulling back.

Over the next week, more American units entered the fray, but the results were similar. At the point of attack, the GIs invariably found themselves outnumbered by a ratio of 10:1 or worse. Further, they lacked high-explosive shells and antitank mines with which to stop the North Koreans' Soviet-built heavy tanks. The Communists steadily drove southward.

On July 13, Lieutenant General Walton Walker, commanding general of the Eighth Army, arrived in Korea. Walker directed his officers to adopt an aggressive posture. American units were to seize every opportunity to counterattack. They were to keep the North Koreans off balance through constant harassment. Walker hoped this would buy him the time he needed.

The 24th Infantry Division, along with ROK forces, dug in behind the meandering Kum River. They delayed the North Korean advance but could not stop it. On July 16, after several days of fighting, the American troops were compelled to withdraw from the Kum River line with heavy casualties. There followed a vicious battle for the city of Taejon, which fell to the North Koreans on July 20. In less than a month, Kim Il Sung's forces had overrun half of South Korea.

The last days of July witnessed dozens of clashes along a front that extended across the breadth of South Korea. As the North Koreans pushed forward relentlessly, General Walker was readying his forces for a do-or-die stand.

Defense of the Pusan Perimeter

The ground Walker planned to defend was a perimeter around the southeastern port city of Pusan. To the west, the perimeter extended about 100 miles northward from the Korea Strait. It then cut eastward some 50 miles to the Sea of Japan.

The terrain offered distinct advantages to the defenders. The northern part of the perimeter ran through rugged mountains. The Naktong River formed an obstacle for the North Koreans along much of the line in the west. Nonetheless, holding the Pusan Perimeter was going to be a dicey proposition for the thinly stretched American and South Korean troops.

In a speech to his division commanders, Walker painted the situation in stark terms. "There is no line behind us," he declared, "to which we can retreat . . . . A retreat to Pusan would be one of the greatest butcheries in history. We must fight until the end."

The fight for the Pusan Perimeter began on August 4. It would rage for six weeks.

The North Koreans broke through the perimeter in multiple places. In the far northeastern corner, they surrounded an ROK division, which had to be evacuated by ship. It rejoined the fight farther south. North Korean divisions crossed the Naktong River in early August. They were beaten back in two weeks of intense fighting.

On the last day of August, the North Koreans began a ferocious, coordinated offensive targeting five separate sectors of the Pusan Perimeter. The attacks punctured the UN lines in several places, and North Korean troops advanced significant distances before being stopped. In the far southwestern corner of the perimeter, Communist forces poured through gaps in positions held by the battered 35th Regiment of the 24th Infantry.

But, with airdropped crates of ammunition, isolated and surrounded American rifle companies clung tenaciously to their hilltop positions for days. This prevented the line from collapsing.

North Korean commanders were growing increasingly desperate to eradicate the Pusan Perimeter. With each passing week, more UN supplies were unloaded, and more troops disembarked, at the port of Pusan. Meanwhile, North Korean supply lines were long and strained. Heavy casualties had depleted North Korean fighting strength. Most of the army's tanks, and much of its artillery, had been destroyed. UN air forces—principally American but now also including British—took a devastating toll.

For the North Korean high command, though, all of that was overshadowed by one inescapable fact. If Pusan didn't fall, UN forces would soon be in a position to mount a counteroffensive.

 TEXT-DEPENDENT QUESTIONS

1. Name the Soviet leader who approved North Korea's invasion of South Korea.
2. What did Security Council Resolution 83 request that UN member states do?
3. What was the Pusan Perimeter? Why was it important?

 RESEARCH PROJECT

Mobile Army Surgical Hospital (MASH) units were introduced in the Korean War. Investigate how MASH units functioned, and how they saved the lives of wounded soldiers. See if you can find firsthand accounts of doctors and nurses who worked in a MASH unit.

Chapter 3

From Inchon to the Yalu

The strategic situation in Korea was clear as the summer of 1950 wound down. To take pressure off the Pusan Perimeter, UN forces would have to conduct an *amphibious landing* someplace to the north. This would cut the enemy's supply lines. It would also threaten the North Koreans besieging Pusan with envelopment.

What wasn't clear, though, was where a UN landing should take place. Douglas MacArthur favored Inchon, a port city located on the western coast of Korea, just south of Seoul. The Joint Chiefs of Staff—the heads of the U.S mili-

Supplies are unloaded at Inchon following the successful landings, September 1950. The Inchon invasion was very risky, but it resulted in a decisive victory for the UN forces, placing North Korea on the defensive for the first time.

tary service branches, who serve as advisers to the president—opposed that choice. So did the U.S. Navy and Marines commanders in Korea. A landing at Inchon, in their view, posed too many unnecessary risks.

The channels approaching Inchon were winding and narrow. Wolmido Island, a stronghold connected to the city by a long causeway, commanded the entrance to the harbor. At Inchon itself, troops couldn't go ashore and move inland on beaches. Instead, the men would have to scale seawalls at the water's edge. Most daunting of all were the extreme tides. The water level dropped more than 30 feet between high and low tide. Wolmido Island would have to be assaulted shortly after sunrise, yet the first wave of troops couldn't be reinforced until evening. Similarly, while the mainland couldn't be attacked until evening, reinforcements would have to wait until the following morning. So if the initial landings ran into trouble, either on Wolmido or at Inchon proper, disaster could ensue.

Despite all that, MacArthur was insistent. He wanted to liberate Seoul as soon as possible. Plus, he argued, the very immensity of the obstacles to a successful landing at Inchon ensured that the North Koreans would never expect UN forces to strike there. In the end, the Joint Chiefs deferred to MacArthur.

A Stunning Victory

MacArthur tapped the U.S. 1st Marine Division to spearhead the Inchon invasion. More than 260 naval vessels would support the operation.

About 6:30 A.M. on September 15, a battalion of Marines stormed ashore on Wolmido Island. The island's defenses had been softened up by

---

 WORDS TO UNDERSTAND IN THIS CHAPTER

amphibious landing— a military action in which land, sea, and air forces work together to invade enemy territory.

garrison—a permanent military installation; the troops stationed at such an installation.

U.S. Marines use ladders to scale the seawall at "Red Beach," Inchon. The Marine at the top of the ladder is First Lieutenant Baldomero Lopez. He was killed a few moments after this photo was taken, but saved the lives of others in his unit by rolling on a grenade. For his heroism Lopez received a posthumous Medal of Honor.

naval and aerial bombardment, and it took the Marines less than six hours to smash the North Korean *garrison*.

That evening, more units from the 1st Marine Division, along with South Korean marines, landed at two locations in Inchon, codenamed "Red Beach" and "Blue Beach." Resistance was fairly light—North Korean commanders had, in fact, expected UN forces to strike elsewhere—and by nightfall the Marines had secured both beachheads.

The North Koreans belatedly dispatched an armored division to repel the invasion. But UN warplanes spotted the column on the highway from Seoul, and they crippled the tanks with bombing runs.

By the afternoon of September 16, Inchon was in UN hands. South Korean marines were left to mop up scattered resistance as the 1st Marine Division began moving toward Seoul. Meanwhile, a steady stream of equipment and troops—including the U.S. Army's 7th Infantry Division—

was coming ashore at Inchon. Along with the 1st Marines, the 7th Infantry would form the backbone of X Corps. X Corps was one of the UN's principal troop formations.

The Inchon landings had been a stunning success. The city was taken at a cost of about 225 UN personnel dead and some 800 wounded. By contrast, thousands of North Korean troops had been killed or captured. Most important, MacArthur's masterstroke ended Kim Il Sung's dream of conquering South Korea. On September 16, the Eighth Army broke out of the Pusan Perimeter. Fearful of being surrounded, North Korean forces began a headlong retreat northward.

How Far to Go?

The battle for Seoul turned into a vicious, house-to-house fight. By September 26, however, UN forces were in control of the South Korean capital. The following day, the northward-driving Eighth Army linked up with elements of the eastward-moving X Corps. The North Korean army was in shambles.

UN troops fight in the streets of Seoul, September 1950.

UN forces had won a great victory. They'd fulfilled the Security Council's directives: North Korea's aggression had been met and reversed.

Should the matter end there? Should the status quo before June 25 be restored, with the 38th parallel dividing the Democratic People's Republic of Korea from the Republic of Korea? Douglas MacArthur didn't think so. "I intend to destroy and not to drive back the North Korean forces," he'd previously admitted to two top American generals. "I may need to occupy all of North Korea."

American officials decided that North Korean forces should be pursued across the 38th parallel, an idea the United Nations endorsed.

Many of President Truman's top civilian advisers were wary of pushing across the 38th parallel. They worried that the Soviet Union or China would respond by sending troops to defend North Korea, which might trigger an expanded war. Truman's civilian advisers believed that a better way to bring the conflict to a conclusion was simply to demand North Korea's surrender. With his army decimated, they thought, Kim Il Sung would comply rather than risk a full-scale invasion by UN forces.

The Joint Chiefs of Staff, however, sided with MacArthur. They shared his objective of completely destroying North Korea's armed forces. Achieving that objective, they recognized, would most likely require military operations beyond the 38th parallel. But they didn't think that posed an undue risk.

Truman ultimately endorsed the Joint Chiefs' view. MacArthur was given permission to conduct military operations in North Korea, subject to certain conditions. Most crucially, he was to suspend offensive operations and immediately consult with Washington if Soviet or Chinese troops entered the conflict. He was to suspend offensive operations even if the Soviet or Chinese government merely threatened to send troops to North Korea.

The Chinese government did, in fact, issue such a threat. It wasn't communicated directly to American officials—China and the United

States didn't maintain diplomatic relations. But on October 3, the Chinese foreign minister informed India's ambassador in Beijing that if U.S. forces crossed the 38th parallel, China would respond militarily. (ROK troops had already begun moving onto North Korean soil.) The ambassador passed the message to American and British diplomats.

MacArthur dismissed the Chinese warning as a bluff. The U.S. intelligence community concurred.

Into North Korea

MacArthur publicly demanded North Korea's surrender. But he didn't bother to wait for a response. On October 9, the Eighth Army crossed the 38th parallel. It joined ROK units in advancing up the western side of North Korea toward the capital city of Pyongyang. North Korean resistance was limited in scope and thoroughly ineffective. UN forces captured Pyongyang on October 19.

Four days earlier, Truman and MacArthur—along with a few of their aides—had conferred on Wake Island, a remote coral atoll in the Pacific. The president asked about the possibility China might enter the war in Korea. That was highly unlikely, MacArthur said, but in the event it did happen, U.S. air power would ensure that "if the Chinese tried to get down to Pyongyang there would be the greatest slaughter."

As a precaution, the Joint Chiefs of Staff forbade MacArthur to send American troops into any North Korean province that bordered China.

President Truman meets with General Douglas MacArthur on Wake Island, in the Pacific, during the Korean War. As the war progressed, the two American leaders would disagree strongly on the best course of action.

U.S. Marines take shelter behind a tank that is firing on a North Korean position.

But MacArthur had no intention of heeding that directive. He planned to send U.S. forces—along with South Korean and other UN troops—all the way to the Yalu River, which forms the boundary between North Korea and China.

The northern part of the Korean Peninsula widens significantly. It's also covered with rugged mountains. A push to the Yalu would require MacArthur to spread his forces thinly. That wouldn't necessarily present an unacceptable risk—provided UN forces were contending only with the battered and beaten North Koreans. By early November, though, it was evident the Chinese had decided to intervene in the Korean War.

First Contacts with the Chinese

On October 25, an advancing ROK division was attacked and stopped in its tracks near the town of Unsan, some 35 miles northeast of Pyongyang. Several days of fierce fighting ensued. During that time, the South Koreans captured a prisoner who, under interrogation, claimed to be part

U.S. Army medics lift a wounded soldier off a helicopter so they can carry him to a Mobile Army Surgical Hospital for emergency treatment.

of a 10,000-man Chinese army in the area. That information was quickly passed up the UNC chain of command to MacArthur's headquarters in Tokyo. MacArthur's top intelligence officer dismissed the report as implausible. The movement of large numbers of troops from China, he insisted, would have been spotted by UN air forces. In fact, the Chinese marched at night and concealed themselves during the day.

On October 29, the 8th Cavalry Regiment of the U.S. 1st Cavalry Division was deployed to Unsan to relieve the exhausted South Koreans. The fighting at Unsan had since petered out. But two large columns of enemy troops were converging on the area. American troops were about to get their first taste of fighting against the Chinese People's Volunteer Army (CPVA). The "volunteer" part of the name was nonsense—the CPVA was composed of units from China's regular army. But China's political leaders thought maintaining the ruse that the troops weren't fighting at the direction of Beijing would lessen the chances of a war with the United States.

On November 1, more than 20,000 CPVA soldiers engaged about 3,600 U.S. and South Korean troops at Unsan. After nightfall, Chinese troops annihilated the ROK regiment holding the easternmost portion of the UN position. They poured through gaps between the 8th Cavalry's three battalions, attacking the Americans from all sides. Around midnight, the 1st and 2nd Battalions were ordered to pull back, with the 3rd Battalion providing cover.

But it was too late for an orderly retreat. The Americans were already encircled. In the darkness, small groups of men—many of them already wounded—tried to slip through the enemy's net. Many didn't make it.

For the next three days, soldiers of the surrounded 3rd Battalion fought desperately to survive. Troops from the 5th Cavalry Regiment attempted to rescue their comrades, but the Chinese beat them back.

An American aircraft can be seen pulling up as its bombs destroy a section of bridge over the Yalu River, on the border between North Korea and China. UN air forces attempted to prevent the movement of Chinese troops into North Korea by destroying bridges and roadways. Note the bomb craters around the bridge left by previous attacks.

THE AIR WAR

In the first months of the Korean War, the UN Command enjoyed air superiority. North Korea's planes and pilots were simply outclassed by their American counterparts. But in late 1950, the advantage briefly shifted to the Communist side when the Soviet MiG-15 was introduced into the conflict. The MiG-15 ranked as one of the best fighter jets in the world. And it wasn't only Chinese and North Korean pilots who were flying the warplanes. Elite Soviet pilots secretly flew combat missions in MiG-15s painted with the markings of the Chinese or North Korean air force.

Soon, though, the Communist aviators found themselves challenged by American pilots flying another advanced fighter jet, the F-86A Sabre. For the duration of the war, frequent dogfights took place over northwestern North Korea—an area UN aviators called "MiG Alley."

An American pilot has a MiG-15 in his gun sights. The arrival of Soviet-built MiG-15 fighters during November 1950 threatened to wrest control of the skies over Korea away from UN forces. The MiG-15 outclassed all other aircraft then deployed.

The United Nations regained air superiority with the arrival of F-86 Sabres in December 1950. These jets, flown by U.S. pilots who were better trained than the North Koreans and Chinese, proved to be more than a match for the MiG-15.

On November 4, aided by airstrikes, the remnants of the 3rd Battalion finally escaped to the south. Of approximately 800 men in the battalion who'd marched into Unsan, only about 200 came out. Overall, U.S. and South Korean forces suffered about 1,700 casualties in the battle.

"An Entirely New War"

If the sudden appearance of Chinese troops on the battlefield had come as a shock to MacArthur and his staff, the sudden disappearance of those troops was baffling. By November 6, UN aerial reconnaissance could find no signs of the large force that had overrun Unsan. It was as if the Chinese had melted into the nearby mountains.

MacArthur initially appeared shaken by the defeat at Unsan. But he soon dismissed its significance. The number of Chinese soldiers in North Korea, he said, was relatively small. And, he insisted, UN ground troops would crush them while UN air forces prevented reinforcements from crossing the Yalu to enter the fray.

In Washington, members of the Truman administration and the Joint Chiefs of Staff were growing increasingly skeptical of MacArthur's rosy assumptions. "The most elementary caution," Secretary of State Acheson noted, "would seem to warn that [the Chinese] might, indeed probably would, reappear as suddenly and harmfully as they had before." Despite that, MacArthur wasn't ordered to halt the UN advance and establish defensive positions. "We sat around like paralyzed rabbits while MacArthur carried out this nightmare," Acheson recalled.

As the November days grew shorter and colder, UN forces pressed ahead, trudging over snow-covered mountains and crossing frozen rivers in their push toward the Yalu. Overall, resistance was fairly light. Communist forces appeared to be in retreat. But that was part of the trap set by Marshall Peng Dehuai, commander of the Chinese People's Volunteer Army. Peng had 300,000 fresh Chinese troops waiting in the mountains near the Yalu.

On November 21, elements of the U.S. 7th Division reached the Yalu at a place called Hyesanjin. To its left, the 1st Marine Division was still more than 60 miles from the river. Further west still, the Eighth Army also remained at a considerable distance from the Yalu.

MacArthur flew to Korea on November 24. He met with Walton Walker, ordering the Eighth Army's commanding general to advance faster. MacArthur announced the start of an all-out offensive, which he said would finally bring the war to an end. He suggested that American troops would be home by Christmas.

Late the next day, 180,000 Chinese soldiers smashed into the Eighth Army. Two days after that, 120,000 more Chinese troops descended on X Corps.

"We face an entirely new war," MacArthur reported. That was stating the obvious.

 # TEXT-DEPENDENT QUESTIONS

1. U.S. Marines spearheaded a landing at what port city on September 15, 1950?
2. Why did some civilian members of the Truman administration consider it risky for the UNC to move north of the 38th parallel?
3. Where is the Yalu River?

 # RESEARCH PROJECT

Using a library or the Internet, find and read the stories of at least three prisoners of war during the Korean War. What common experiences did the POWs have?

Chapter 4

Offensive and Counteroffensive

The CPVA attack of November 25 was devastating. Under the cover of darkness, Chinese troops crept close to the Eighth Army's frontline units. Then they launched a series of massive frontal assaults. In some places, UN soldiers repulsed four or five human-wave attacks. But regardless of how many men they lost, the Chinese kept coming. Eventually, UN units suffered too many casualties to fight effectively, or they simply ran out of ammunition. Then they were overrun.

After obliterating three South Korean divisions holding the right flank, the

U.S. Marines of the 5th and 7th Regiments, who hurled back a surprise onslaught by three Chinese Communist divisions, wait to withdraw, December 1950.

Chinese tried to encircle the Eighth Army at the Chongchon River. The UN forces escaped, but not without major losses. Especially hard hit was the 2nd Infantry Division. As it pulled back, the division fell into a huge ambush on the only road through a mountain gorge.

General Walker soon found himself trying to engineer a fighting retreat. It was the only way he could save the Eighth Army.

The Chosin Reservoir Campaign

If anything, the situation to the east was even more desperate. On November 27, the Chinese attacked in force around the frozen Changjin Reservoir, located in a desolate area of the forbidding Taebaek Mountains. By November 29, the 1st Marine Division and elements of the 7th Infantry Division were surrounded, and Chinese forces held the high ground.

"The annihilation of the United States 1st Marine Division," China's official government radio station confidently predicted, "is only a matter of time." In fact, the action that began around the Chosin Reservoir (as UN forces called the man-made lake) would become one of the most storied chapters in the annals of the United States Marine Corps.

Some of the credit belongs to the 1st Marine Division's commander, Major General Oliver Smith. Smith considered a rapid push to the Yalu reckless. Bucking MacArthur's wishes, he'd moved the 1st Marine Division cautiously. He'd even paused the division's advance while his engineers constructed an airstrip and base to the south of the Changjin Reservoir.

Still, only feats of extraordinary determination, endurance, and valor could save the UN forces at Changjin. For five nights and four days, a sin-

 WORDS TO UNDERSTAND IN THIS CHAPTER

insubordination—disobedience of authority; a refusal to obey orders.
napalm—a highly flammable, sticky jelly that is used in incendiary
    bombs.

U.S. Marines move forward after napalm dropped from a UN aircraft flushes out the Chinese from their hillside entrenchment near Hagaru-ri, December 1950.

gle Marine company, numbering fewer than 250 men, defended a key hill against a 10,000-man Chinese division. This allowed thousands of other Marines and soldiers to pull back to Hagaru-ri, at the southern tip of the reservoir. From there, the UN forces battled southward 11 miles to the Marine base at Koto-ri.

Safety still lay more than 60 miles to the southeast, at the port city of Hungnam. But, led by the Marines and fighting through ice, snow, and temperatures that sometimes plummeted to -35°F, the UN troops hammered away at the Chinese divisions blocking their way. All the while, they held at bay enemy divisions trying to engulf them from the rear.

At one point, the UN column appeared trapped after the Chinese blew up the bridge across a 1,500-foot gorge. However, Marine combat engineers assembled a new bridge from sections airdropped by American cargo planes.

Within the first few months of the Korean War, American bombers like this B-29 had destroyed or damaged most of the industrial targets in North Korea.

On December 11, Marine rearguard units arrived in Hungnam. Two and a half weeks of fighting had taken a heavy toll. Some 3,000 UN troops had been killed, and about twice that number wounded. Thousands more suffered frostbite. But Chinese dead and wounded from the Chosin Reservoir campaign totaled at least 35,000, with an additional 25,000 or more incapacitated by frostbite.

Most important, X Corps hadn't been destroyed. About 100,000 UN troops were evacuated by sea from Hungnam. More than 90,000 Korean refugees joined them. The evacuation was completed on Christmas Eve.

Command Issues

The Eighth Army, meanwhile, had retreated to a line approximately 25 miles north of Seoul. Its commander, General Walton Walker, was killed in a jeep accident on December 23. He would be replaced by General Matthew Ridgway.

In the month since China's entry into the war, the UNC's air campaign had intensified. It targeted not only enemy troops, but also, by MacArthur's orders, every "installation, factory, city, and village" in Communist-controlled North Korea. High-explosive bombs and *napalm* reduced many areas to rubble and ash, killing countless civilians.

But MacArthur wanted to further expand the scope of the air campaign. He requested permission to bomb targets inside China. He even asked for the authority to use nuclear weapons in Korea as he deemed necessary, submitting a list of potential targets and requesting 26 atomic bombs.

It's impossible to know how MacArthur's proposed course of action would have played out. China lacked nuclear weapons and otherwise had little capacity to retaliate against the United States directly. But how would the Soviet Union respond? In 1950, it was the only nuclear-armed nation besides the United States.

In any case, President Truman rejected MacArthur's requests. Truman was determined to prevent the conflict from expanding beyond the Korean Peninsula.

MacArthur was unhappy. How could the war be won if Chinese forces were allowed sanctuary just beyond the Yalu River? The prohibition on attacking Chinese troops and bases in Manchuria, MacArthur complained in a magazine interview, was "an enormous handicap, without precedent in military history." For good measure, the general released his remarks to a news agency. This ensured they would be covered in major American newspapers.

MacArthur's comments amounted to thinly veiled criticism of the Truman administration's Korea policy. Truman and his advisers bristled. In the American system, the president is commander-in-chief of the armed forces. In wartime, the president (often in consultation with Congress) determines the overall direction of the nation's war effort, including specific goals. The president may restrict which weapons are used or decide that certain targets are off-limits. Military leaders are expected to follow the president's orders. Believing that MacArthur was openly undermining his authority, Truman prohibited any leader in the U.S. armed forces from publicly discussing foreign policy or military policy without prior approval from the State Department. MacArthur, however, would flout that order on several occasions.

A Turning Point

On the last day of 1950, the Chinese launched a renewed offensive. By January 4, 1951, Seoul had once again fallen to the Communists. The following day, UN forces abandoned Inchon. Soon they'd fallen back to a line about 40 miles south of Seoul.

MacArthur informed the Joint Chiefs that, given the restrictions the Truman administration had placed on him, the Eighth Army's position couldn't be sustained. The army would either be driven from the Korean Peninsula, he indicated, or it would be destroyed.

 # INTEGRATING THE MILITARY

For much of the nation's history, the U.S. armed forces maintained a policy of racial segregation. African Americans who donned the uniform were typically consigned to all-black units.

In 1948, President Truman issued an executive order requiring the armed forces to desegregate. Some white soldiers—particularly from the South—objected, and the military establish-

An African-American sergeant points out North Korean positions to his integrated machine-gun squad, 1950.

ment was slow to comply with Truman's order. When the Korean War broke out, the Eighth Army was still racially segregated. During the first desperate months of fighting, however, many depleted units began accepting whatever replacement GIs were available, regardless of race. Unit cohesion didn't suffer, and in May 1951 General Matthew Ridgway officially abolished segregation among the American forces in Korea.

This map shows the Communist offensive of early 1951. South Korean and UN forces retreated southward on the Korean Peninsula. The Communist offensive stalled when heavily outnumbered American and French forces held off a Chinese army at Chipyong-ni in February 1951.

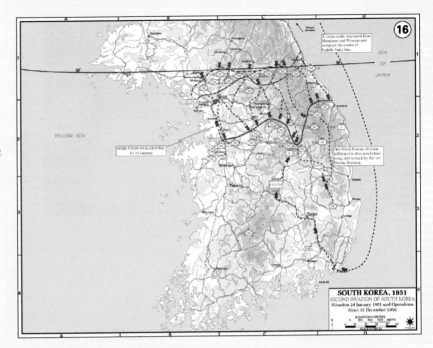

The Eighth Army's commander on the ground didn't share that assessment. In late January, General Matthew Ridgway began a large probing action, in preparation for a major counteroffensive. UN forces first moved forward in the west, below Seoul. Then the attack was gradually extended eastward. Resistance was mostly light, because the Chinese were resupplying. By February 10, UN forces had advanced an average of about 20 miles across the breadth of the peninsula.

The following day, however, the Chinese struck heavily at the center of the front. ROK divisions were driven south toward the city of Wonju.

Ridgway ordered the U.S. 2nd Infantry Division's 23rd Regiment to hold the town of Chipyong-ni (now called Jipyeong-ri), an important transportation hub northwest of Wonju. The 23rd Regiment was bolstered by a battalion of French soldiers. In all, though, there were only about 5,600 UNC troops at Chipyong-ni. Against this force, the Chinese threw an army of 25,000 men. In desperate fighting, the American and French troops held on from February 13 until February 15, when elements of the 5th Cavalry Regiment arrived and the Chinese withdrew.

The battle at Chipyong-ni marked a turning point. The Communist offensive had been broken. Chinese forces began pulling back throughout

A few days after being relieved of command in Korea, General MacArthur delivered a nationally televised speech to Congress, defending his actions in Korea. Today, most historians agree that Truman made the right decision in dismissing MacArthur.

the central part of the front.

Ridgway's counteroffensive was soon in full swing. UN forces made steady progress. By March 15, Seoul had been recaptured.

MacArthur Relieved of Command

Momentum in the war had shifted to the UNC, whose forces were approaching the 38th parallel. Truman believed the Chinese might now be open to a negotiated settlement of the conflict.

On March 20, the Joint Chiefs informed MacArthur that the president would soon be floating a cease-fire offer. MacArthur preempted the president's announcement by issuing his own, unauthorized statement to the Chinese. He disparaged Chinese fighting ability and threatened an expansion of the war into China if the Communists didn't come to peace terms.

The statement was a stunning act of *insubordination*, and it sabotaged Truman's peace initiative before it had even been rolled out. Then, in early April, a Massachusetts congressman (and vocal critic of Truman) made public a brief letter MacArthur had written to him. In it, the general criticized the administration's approach to fighting communism and endorsed the idea of using Nationalist Chinese troops to help fight the Chinese Communists. Truman had finally had enough. On April 11, he sacked MacArthur. General Ridgway was elevated to commander-in-chief of the United Nations Command. Lieutenant General James A. Van Fleet assumed command of the Eighth Army.

Deadlock Around the 38th Parallel

By mid-April, UN forces had advanced to what was called the Kansas Line. It ran slightly below the 38th parallel in the far western part of Korea, and slightly above across the rest of the peninsula. Taking advantage of land features, Ridgway intended to fortify the Kansas Line so that it would be virtually invulnerable to attack.

Before that could be accomplished, though, the Chinese and North Koreans launched another major offensive. Lasting from April 22 to May 20, the offensive succeeded in pushing UN forces back across the 38th parallel. But it failed in one of its major objectives—recapturing Seoul.

More important, when the Communists paused to resupply, Van Fleet immediately unleashed a counterattack by the Eighth Army. At the end of the UN's May 22–July 8 offensive, UN forces once again held the Kansas Line.

A U.S. Marine guards Chinese soldiers captured during the UN offensive in March 1951 to regain control of Seoul.

Peace talks began on July 10 in Kaesong, a small city just south of the 38th parallel. The talks quickly bogged down.

The war would drag on for another two years, but the outcome was no longer in doubt: Korea would remain divided into two countries. Recognizing that strategic reality, neither side would mount another all-out offensive for the rest of the war. Nevertheless, many more lives would be expended in savage fighting for hills, ridges, and other tactically important ground in the vicinity of the 38th parallel.

TEXT-DEPENDENT QUESTIONS

1. What was the name of the man-made lake where Chinese forces seemed to have the 1st Marine Division trapped in late November and early December 1950?
2. Why did President Truman fire General MacArthur?
3. Who succeeded MacArthur as head of the UN Command?

RESEARCH PROJECT

How do you think the country reacted to MacArthur's dismissal? Would you guess that a) most Americans agreed with Truman's decision; b) most Americans opposed Truman's decision; or c) public opinion was evenly divided? Use library or Internet resources to check your guess. Did anything you discovered surprise you?

Chapter 5

Die for a Tie?

In late August 1951, the Communists walked out of the peace talks in Kaesong. By this time, it was clear that the war in Korea was settling into a *stalemate*.

Rank-and-file American troops now understood that there would be no decisive victory in Korea. The war would not end with a Communist surrender. It would end—eventually—when the two sides' negotiators hammered out an agreement. And Communists would remain in power in North Korea. Many GIs

President-elect Dwight D. Eisenhower (second from left) reviews UN troops in South Korea, November 1952. During the 1952 election campaign, Eisenhower, a highly respected former military leader, had promised to visit Korea and get a firsthand look at the situation. Convinced that the war in Korea could not be won by either side, as president he insisted on

The fiercely contested hill known as Heartbreak Ridge is visible in this photo taken along the mountainous 38th parallel in 1951. The constant fighting in this area created a treeless landscape similar to the trench lines of World War I.

found that difficult to accept. Their frame of reference was World War II, in which the United States and its allies had achieved total victory. In Korea, the troops said bitterly, the watchword was "die for a tie."

Lessons from Heartbreak Ridge

The eastern sector of the front would see heavy fighting in the late summer and early fall of 1951. In the rugged Taebaek Mountains, General Van Fleet wanted to eliminate a salient in the UN lines near a basin American troops called the Punchbowl.

To the west of the Punchbowl, UN troops drove North Korean and Chinese troops off a line of hills dubbed Bloody Ridge. But the Communists retrenched on high ground less than a mile to the north. It would become known to Americans as Heartbreak Ridge.

 WORDS TO UNDERSTAND IN THIS CHAPTER

armistice—an agreement to suspend hostilities; a truce.
stalemate—a situation in which neither side in a conflict or contest can gain an advantage that enables them to win.

From September 13 to October 15, UN forces battled to dislodge the enemy from well-fortified positions on Heartbreak Ridge. Much of the fighting consisted of hand-to-hand combat. In many cases, UN infantry troops—mostly Americans and French—clawed their way to the top of a rocky slope, only to be swept back down by a counterattack. When the month-long battle was over, Heartbreak Ridge was in UN hands. But UN forces had suffered about 3,700 casualties.

Many officers in the UNC wondered whether such high casualties could still be justified in the pursuit of modest tactical goals. Ridgway soon instructed Van Fleet to discontinue major offensive operations and pursue an "active defense"—that is, to hold territory through counterattacks and, where necessary, limited offensive action. For the most part, UNC ground forces adopted an active-defense posture for the remainder of the war.

A Truce Too Long in Coming

Peace talks resumed in late October 1951. The venue had been changed, to the small village of Panmunjom, but the results were the same: an agreement proved elusive.

In 1952, in an attempt to pressure Communist negotiators into making concessions at Panmunjom, the UNC began a stepped-up bombing campaign in North Korea. In many areas, cities and villages were so thoroughly devastated that people survived by living in caves. When UNC warplanes ran out of urban targets, they started bombing hydroelectric dams.

U.S. members of the UN delegation to the armistice conference attend a daily meeting at Panmunjom. Navy Vice Admiral C. Turner Joy, serving as chief delegate, is at the center left.

General W.K. Harrison of the U.S. Army (left table) and North Korea's General Nam Il (right table) sign the armistice documents, July 27, 1953.

For their part, the Chinese and North Koreans sought to gain leverage at Panmunjom by demonstrating their willingness to continue inflicting—and absorbing—heavy casualties with large ground attacks on UN positions. But neither side budged, and the peace talks broke up in October 1952 without making any progress.

Another winter of bitter fighting followed. When negotiators came back to the table in April 1953, Communist and American forces were engaged in an intense struggle over a UN outpost known as Pork Chop Hill. The fighting there would rage for months. Meanwhile, UN aerial bombing became even more pitiless. North Korean irrigation dams were targeted. This caused devastating flooding and destroyed the spring rice crop, bringing the specter of mass starvation.

In the midst of these horrors, the talks at Panmunjom finally bore fruit. On July 27, 1953, an **armistice** was signed, marking an end to the fighting.

Losses and Legacies

All told, it's estimated that the three-year-long Korean War claimed the lives of some 3 million people, about half of them civilians. Millions of others were wounded or maimed. What's remarkable about that sickening toll is how little it altered the political situation on the Korean Peninsula, at least in the short term. After the war, Kim Il Sung remained in power in North Korea, just as Syngman Rhee remained in power in South Korea. The border between the two countries remained very close to where it had been when the war started. The antagonisms that led to the war were never resolved. Indeed, the war never technically ended, as North and South Korea didn't conclude a peace treaty.

According to the U.S. Department of Defense, 36,574 Americans lost their lives in the Korean War. More than 100,000 others were wounded. Had they suffered and sacrificed, bled and died for "a tie"? Yes, but that's essentially what the original goal of the UN intervention was: to roll back North Korean aggression, not to vanquish North Korea. The Truman administration also recognized that, after MacArthur's ill-advised push to the Yalu, a deadlock was the best attainable outcome. Communism could be contained on the Korean Peninsula. But it couldn't be eliminated without the risk of triggering a wider—and potentially cataclysmic—conflict.

Today, South Korea is a vibrant, prosperous nation with a stable democracy. Isolated, impoverished North Korea, meanwhile, has one of the world's most repressive governments—a brutal Communist dictatorship helmed by the grandson of Kim Il Sung. It's not difficult to imagine that South Koreans also would be living that nightmare if not for the Americans who fought in "the Forgotten War."

 ## TEXT-DEPENDENT QUESTIONS

1. What was the total number of UN casualties at Heartbreak Ridge?
2. What took place at the small village of Panmunjom?

 ## RESEARCH PROJECT

Prepare a timeline of significant events that have occurred on the Korean Peninsula after the end of the Korean War. List events in North Korea on one side of the line, and events in South Korea on the opposite side.

Chronology

1945   Following the surrender of Japan in World War II, Soviet and American officials agree to the temporary division of Korea at a latitude of 38°N.

1948   UN-sponsored elections lead to the establishment of the Republic of Korea (South Korea), with Syngman Rhee as its president. A rival Communist state, the Democratic People's Republic of Korea, is proclaimed in North Korea; it's headed by Kim Il Sung.

1950   June: The Korean War begins on June 25 when North Korean forces invade South Korea. Two days later, the United Nations authorizes member states to contribute military forces to help South Korea repel the invasion.

July: General Douglas MacArthur is appointed commander-in-chief of the UN Command. American troops begin arriving in Korea.

August: Defense of the Pusan Perimeter begins.

September–October: A UN offensive, which begins with an amphibious landing at Inchon (Sept. 15), drives the North Koreans back across the 38th parallel. In late October, Chinese forces enter fighting near Unsan.

November–December: A Chinese offensive begins with massive attacks on Eighth Army (Nov. 25) and X Corps (Nov. 27). 1st Marine Division leads epic fighting retreat from Changjin (Chosin) Reservoir to Hungnam.

1951   February: Chinese momentum is finally broken at Chipyong-ni, in the central part of the front. Eighth Army launches a counterattack.

1951 March: MacArthur issues an unauthorized statement to the Chinese, sabotaging a cease-fire proposal planned by Truman.

April–July: Truman relieves MacArthur of command (April 11); Matthew Ridgway becomes commander-in-chief of UNC. Major Communist offensive (April 22–May 20) drives UN forces from Kansas Line and back across the 38th parallel. Eighth Army counteroffensive (May 22–July 8) regains Kansas Line. Peace talks begin July 10 at Kaesong.

August: Communists walk out of peace talks.

September–October: Battle of Heartbreak Ridge. Peace talks resume at Panmunjom.

1952 Each side tries to pressure the other to accept concessions at the peace talks—the UNC by intensifying bombing in North Korea, the Communists by launching a series of ground attacks designed to inflict heavy casualties. But peace talks are suspended indefinitely in October.

1953 Bloody battles (such as the Battle of Pork Chop Hill) joined in the spring. Peace talks resume in April. An armistice is finally signed on July 27.

Chapter Notes

p. 10:   "This was an all-out war," Rich Shopes, " 'Korean Conflict' Tag Gets Boot in Favor of New Wording," *Tampa Bay Times*, June 19, 2014. http://www.tampabay.com/news/politics/legislature/korean-conflict-tags-get-boot-in-favor-of-new-designation/2185152

p. 11:   "completely and forever," "The Annexation of Korea," *Japan Times*, August 29, 2010. http://www.japantimes.co.jp/opinion/2010/08/29/editorials/the-annexation-of-korea/#.VSLFs_nF-H4

p. 20:   "So far as the military . . ." Dean Acheson, *Present at the Creation: My Years in the State Department*. Reprint. (New York: W. W. Norton & Co., 1987), p. 357.

p. 20:   "the initial reliance . . ." Ibid.

p. 21:   "If you should get kicked . . ." David Halberstam, *The Coldest Winter: America and the Korean War* (New York: Hyperion, 2007), p. 50.

p. 24:   "furnish such assistance . . ." Security Council Resolutions, "Complaint of aggression upon the Republic of Korea," 83 (1950). Resolution of 27 June 1950. http://www.un.org/en/ga/search/view_doc.asp?symbol=S/RES/83(1950)

p. 24:   "The attack upon Korea ..." Harry S. Truman, "Statement by the President on the Situation in Korea," June 27, 1950. Harry S. Truman Presidential Library, http://www.trumanlibrary.org/publicpapers/viewpapers.php?pid=800

p. 25:   "If the best minds . . ." Halberstam, *The Coldest Winter*, p. 1.

p. 29:   "There is no line . . ." Bill McWilliams, *On Hallowed Ground: The Last Battle for Pork Chop Hill* (Annapolis, MD: Naval Institute Press, 2004), p. 9.

p. 35:   "I intend to destroy . . ." Alex Roberto Hybel, *U.S. Foreign Policy Decision-Making from Truman to Kennedy: Responses to International Challenges* (New York: Palgrave Macmillan, 2014), p. 72.

p. 36:   "if the Chinese tried . . ." Max Hastings, *The Korean War* (New York: Simon & Schuster, 1988), p. 123.

p. 41:   "The most elementary caution . . ." Halberstam, *The Coldest Winter*, p. 44.

p. 41:   "We sat around . . ." Ibid.

p. 42:   "We face an entirely . . ." Acheson, *Present at the Creation*, p. 469.

p. 44:   "The annihilation . . ." James Wright, *Those Who Have Borne the Battle: A History of America's Wars and Those Who Fought Them* (New York: PublicAffairs, 2012) p. 142.

p. 47:   "installation, factory, . . ." Bruce Cumings, *The Korean War: A History* (New York: Modern Library, 2010), p. 29.

p. 47:   "an enormous handicap . . ." Michael D. Pearlman, *Truman and MacArthur: Policy, Politics, and the Hunger for Honor and Renown* (Bloomington: Indiana University Press, 2008), p. 170.

Further Reading

Behnke, Alison. *Kim Jong Il's North Korea*. Minneapolis: Lerner, 2008.

Cumings, Bruce. *The Korean War: A History*. New York: Modern Library, 2010.

Halberstam, David. *The Coldest Winter: America and the Korean War*. New York: Hyperion, 2007.

Pash, Melinda L. *In the Shadow of the Greatest Generation: The Americans Who Fought the Korean War*. New York: NYU Press, 2012.

Rice, Earle, Jr. *Korea 1950: Pusan to Chosin*. Broomall, PA: Chelsea House, 2003.

Weintraub, Stanley. *A Christmas Far from Home: An Epic Tale of Courage and Survival During the Korean War*. Boston: Da Capo Press, 2014.

Yancey, Diane. *Korean War: The Life of an American Soldier*. San Diego: Lucent, 2003.

Internet Resources

www.trumanlibrary.org/whistlestop/study_collections/koreanwar/index.php
The Harry S. Truman Library and Museum maintains this site, "The Korean War and Its Origins, 1945–1953." It features documents, images, and audio clips.

http://www.koreanwar60.com
Home page of the Department of Defense 60th Anniversary of Korean War Commemoration Committee.

http://www.history.army.mil/reference/Korea/kw-chrono.htm
A timeline of the Korean War, from the U.S. Army Center of Military History.

http://koreanwar.democratandchronicle.com/
The *Democrat and Chronicle* (Rochester, NY) offers a collection of fascinating photographs from the Korean War.

Index

Numbers in **bold italics** refer to captions.

SERIES GLOSSARY

blockade—an effort to cut off supplies, war material, or communications by a particular area, by force or the threat of force.

guerrilla warfare—a type of warfare in which a small group of combatants, such as armed civilians, use hit-and-run tactics to fight a larger and less mobile traditional army. The purpose is to weaken an enemy's strength through small skirmishes, rather than fighting pitched battles where the guerrillas would be at a disadvantage.

intelligence—the analysis of information collected from various sources in order to provide guidance and direction to military commanders.

logistics—the planning and execution of movements by military forces, and the supply of those forces.

salient—a pocket or bulge in a fortified line or battle line that projects into enemy territory.

siege—a military blockade of a city or fortress, with the intent of conquering it at a later stage.

tactics—the science and art of organizing a military force, and the techniques for using military units and their weapons to defeat an enemy in battle.